A Light Shining Through

Jessica Hardin

BookLeaf Publishing

India | USA | UK

Presentation by *BookLeaf Publishing*

Web: www.bookleafpub.com

E-mail: info@bookleafpub.com

ISBN: 9789358318098

First edition 2023

DEDICATION

This book is dedicated to my wonderful husband and children, who I am so grateful to for being a source of strength and encouragement on this journey. I also dedicate this book to God for giving me the ability to write and for being a light shining through.

ACKNOWLEDGEMENT

I would like to thank my parents for raising me to love the word of God and my husband and my children for encouraging and supporting me to follow my inspiration to write this book.

PREFACE

It's when it's the darkest that we seek for the light. We fumble around lost and blind looking for the slightest glimmer to illuminate the way. We struggle to put one foot in front of the other and not fall grabbing ahold to whatever we can to keep our balance. We get so used to the darkness that it becomes a covering we wrap ourselves in, a safe place to hide. So much so that we wouldn't notice a sliver of light peeking through. Weve learned to hate and love the darkness, but we still can't see our way, so we call out for the light and suddenly a slight streak of light comes shining through. It's in this moment as we welcome the warm glow of the light that we come to the realization that as much as we longed for such brightness, indeed without the darkness we would not know what light is.

Thats what the poem's in this book is about finding your way out of the darkness by a single glimmer of hope, a light shining through. For me that light represents the redeeming power of God in my life. In a time when I felt lost, I found my hope in God, and he lit my way much as Psalms 119:105 says " Your word is a lamp to my feet and a light to my path."

A Thorn In My Flesh

What is this anxious craving?
gnawing away at my bones
crashing over me like breaking waves
in thunderous overtones
what is this wretched feeling clawing at me deep
within?
sharpening its monstrous grip over and over
again
it shakes me out of bed.
and terrifies my sleep.
it stalks the thoughts in my head and into
memories does creep.
I try to push it away, but it fights its way to me.
Once I become its prisoner and it's got me in its
grasp
then it will leave me be for a while until my next
lapse
Then it will come back fresh and anew
this thorn in my flesh
that I cut but it grew

Addiction

A nagging obsession tells you need it.
brainwashes you into believing the lie every
time you feed it.
comes with no warning and an incredible urge.
A daunting desire to devour and purge.
screams from the rooftops and blares in the
streets.
shouts above the crowd to everyone it greets and
makes false promises to everyone it meets.
runs like fire through your veins.
and doesn't care who it claims.
not easily recognizable, it goes by many
different names.

At The Altar

A whisper in the air
a salty summer breeze.
lingers around me and puts me at ease.
like warm sunshine on my skin
like standing too close to a fire
I am heated within and filled with desire.
Weak kneed and faint
I walk slowly.
fist balled up with hate.
I long to be holy.
tears fall like snowflakes that stick to your skin.
past every pew
carrying my sin
that welcoming warmth is getting brighter.
with every step I take I feel lighter
it beckons to me.
and I pray not to falter.
as i reach a place of peace.
and lay it all at the altar.

Saved

You heard my cry's.
 you saw my tears.
you rescued me from all my fears.
you held my hand.
you kissed my cheek.
you gave me strength when I was weak.
you picked me up
you held me close
you were there when I needed you most.
you gave me love
you gave me grace
when push came to shove
you pled my case
you walked me away from the arms of
condemption
and into your freedom without as much as a
mention
You gave me faith
You rescued my soul
Such mercy
You saved me and made me whole

Alcoholism

Targeting Ravenous and insatiable the hunger
within

 every weak moment in order to devour and sin

Eating away at whatever confidence is left or
has been

Like a corrosion deep and without end

It penetrates the mind and numbs it

Calls forth a world not so serious and trumps it

But there is a world of reality left still to defend

There's a fine line between safe and sober

When we close our eyes

And say our prayers with a bottle pressed
against our lips in beautiful disguise

The swirling colors alluring scent track us down
and drag us in

The threat real but invisible

One step closer to heaven or hell and miserable

While we play grownups and fall away to a
discontented state

Where indifference is the norm and we can't
recognize love from hate

 Remorse is too close to discomfort and not
close enough to repentance

Denial is empty and so is the next sentence

Anger is inevitable and so is prideful resistance

Where is hope in a world so cold?

You fight to rid the ice around you just so you
can be told

That your best punch isn't good enough you'll
never break its hold

You're sick of starting over pushing doubt and
fear away again

You've made faith an enemy and disappointment
a friend

Nothing to look to nothing to look towards

But you keep holding the promise that the battle
is the Lords

Waiting

Anxious thoughts
Overwhelming feelings
A heart in need of healing
Racing images in a blur
Insecurities that raise their ugly head occur
Siting,waiting, praying, pacing
A familiarness I fear facing
Straining to hear your voice
Frustrated at the silence all around
Trying to make the right choice and talk myself
down
Standing on your promises
Standing on your word
Searching for answers in the bible
Faith in the message I heard all the while
Eyes closed tight I now my head and nod
And a voice of power and might said
Be still and know that I am God

Overcoming

I've tried, I've tried
I've failed
And I've tried again
Each time wears me down a little more
It's exhausting my efforts
And making them thin
I cry out for help
I know deliverance is near
I call out your name
You draw your presence here
But I am still troubled
Pressures are acting out of long set preconceived
notions
That the world is somehow against me
And I'm drowning in it's oceans
You have overcome the world
With all that's conceived of sin
You have overcome those things
That rest heavy on the hearts of men
So why do I feel
The sting
The pain
The hurt of a memory again
As if it was yesterday
Embedded within

If today I have grown even an inch closer
To your glory
Then
What you say is good enough
To rescue me
From all worry
You've already taken my sin

Big God

There's something so beautiful about a summer
sunset
Something so pure in a soft gentle breeze
That we as humans just don't get
Like the rustling of autumn leaves
Something so magnificent about the mountains
in all their glory and splendor
Something so wondrous nature can't hinder
Something so serene in the ripples of a trickling
spring
Something so peaceful it makes the earth sing
and carry it's melody on eagles wings
Something so soft about the flowers in the field
and something so cleansing about a gentle rain
That only God could ever build and give each
one it's name.
Something so fierce about the ocean waves that
crash upon shore and something so powerful
about the rattling thunder
That leaves the universe forever in wonder
Something so tender about a doe with its fawn
something so radiant about about a sun rise
That even the dusk envies the brilliance of the
dawn and the moon envies having to share the
sky's

No man could duplicate the works of the
almighty's hand
No man could count the stars or measure the
grains of sand
No man could hold the universe in their palm or
separates the seas from land and make them
calm
No one but God, no one but the great I am
Could tear down this world and rebuild it again
But God can and someday will
We serve a big God and he's big still

Ninety nine

I know he leaves the ninety nine to find the one I
know he calls and searches until the hunt is done
I know he listens for the bleating of the ones
who's lost, he grabs his staff and runs after them
determined to bring them back whatever the
cost. He looks for the one who veered off
course the one who ran away so that he can
rescue them and give them green pastures to lay.
He never gets angry, he never changes his mind,
he pushes on ahead until he's returned the one he
seeked out to find. Hell fight any enemy who
stands between him and that one
he wins every battle
And the wars already won
I know he leaves the ninety nine to find the one
He pursues until he catches up and takes them
back to the fold,
He wraps them in his living arms and shelters
them from the cold
He puts them up on his shoulders and carries
them back
Where they'll have everything they need and
never lack
I know he leaves the ninety nine to find the one
if only one is all there is

I know he leaves the ninety nine to find the one
because their his
I know he leaves the ninety nine to find the one
no matter how long the search may be
I know he leaves the ninety nine to find the one
and that one was me

He knows my name

God, do you see me
God, do you hear me
Am I getting through
Or do my prayers stop short at heavens gate
waiting on you
God, are you there
God, do you know
God this feeling
is like my prayers can't make it past the ceiling
God are you listening
Where are you at
Are you gone
When are you coming back
Are you busy
Are you sleeping
Are you watching with your great eye
Are words too much for heaven to contain
Should I even try
Just then I heard God whisper my name
And I began to cry
I new in that moment I was seen I was heard that
my prayers were answered before I ever said a
word
And I thanked God for hearing me out
And asked for forgiveness for my fear and doubt

Now when I'm tempted to ask if your there
Ill remember that you know my name and I'll
just say a prayer

No reason to worry

He tells the bears when to hibernate and the lion
where to gets his prey,
He helps the tiger birth it's young
And gives them a place to lay
He helps the birds make their nest and gives
them their song to sing
He gives the dolphin its flippers to swim and
gives the the eagle it's wings
He helps the squirrels gather their nuts
And tell the geese where to fly for the winter
He protects and corrects the saint and the sinner
He waters the grass and makes the plants grow
He blooms flowers and red and blue
And makes the stars glow
If this is how he takes care of all creation
Then he can surely take care of me
There's no reason now or ever
To worry

Never gave up on me

I thought you were mad
I thought you were angry
Sick of my failures
Frustrated at me
I wondered if you'd grown too tired and your
patience thin
I'm sure you were disappointed in my behavior
But then
I remembered you love the sinner but hate the
sin, your my savior
Thank you for never giving up on me
For not letting me give in
When I felt hopeless
I found my hope in him
When I couldn't even lift my eyes
Too ashamed to meet your glance
you showed up and gave me another chance
Thank goodness for your love your grace and
mercy
Without it don't know where id be

The struggle

Some days it seems like I'm doing alright
Like Ill make it through ok
But no one knows the fright of if I cant
And how it never goes away
I try to be strong , carry on and do my best
But the truth is every day is a test
I constantly wonder if its something I'm able to
beat
But I keep my faith in God that it's something I
can defeat
Its gotten easier
But I don't know if it will ever be gone
Will I ever sing a new tune or just the same old
song

Overwhelmed

I feel like I'm being pulled in every direction but
mine
Running out of energy and running out of time
There's things to be done
Too many to count
Im stressed and then some a considerable
amount
The list just goes on
So much to do
I'm lacking motivation and energy too
My heads all a mess
I can think straight
I feel like my efforts are all in vain and second
rate
Every body needs or wants something and I'm
only one person
I can't make everyone happy
My anxiety is bursting
But it will be ok
I'll take one thing at a time
I'm just a little overwhelmed today

Blessed

I may not be rich
Or drive a fancy car
Dress in emeralds and rubies
Or take trips afar
But I got the morals my moma raised me with
And that is more than I can say
For the majority of folks today
I may not own land
Or yaught
But I know what's right
And I know what's not
I know the good manners and respect I was
taught
I still believe in tradition
And doing what's right
I believe in the bible and standing to fight
I believe in solid principals
I believe in peace
I believe in being kind at the least
I believe in giving grace
And doing a good deed
I may not have everything the world says I
should but I have everything I need
I have what's important
Yes indeed

I have a roof over my head and food to eat
I have a shirt on my back and shoes on my feet
I have love and laughter
I have forgiveness
I have what matters
Forget all the rest
I have much to be grateful for
I'm blessed
I have faith
And hope is a must
My children love God and Jesus
What else could I ask for
I have everything and so much more

On my way

I'm not perfect
Never pretended to be
Sometimes I forget how far I've come
In order to be free
Some days I take two steps forward and three
steps back
I'm not where I want to be thank God I'm not
where I was at
Some days are harder than others
But I'm better than I have been in a long while
Some days ok
Others a trial
But I'm slowly gaining ground
And I'm growing every day
I'm not where I want to be
But I'm on my way

He's still on the throne

This world is a mess
I look around and all I see
Is the world trying to keep people down
Who are doing their best to live happy and free
Too much political propaganda
How do you know what to believe
The world needs more Jesus
Less voices to deceive
The TV and the radio can fill you with fear
But God is still on the throne
His rule is still clear
There's too much misdirection
The whole world seems confused
Too many reasons to stay divided
No matter what you choose
Too much controversy
And we've all but forgotten we the people
Church has become just a building with a steeple
But God is still in charge
He has the last say
He is still sovereign in each and every way
People have become blind, deaf and dumb
Concerned with earthly matters
when there's really only one
And that's to be ready when Jesus comes back

But until then he's still on the throne
That's a fact

Blessed

I may not be rich
Or drive a fancy car
Dress in emralds and rubies
Or take trips afar
But I got the morals my moma raised me with
And that is more than I can say
For the majority of folks today
I may not own land
Or yaught
But I know what's right
And I know what's not
I know the good manners and respect I was
taught
I still believe in tradition
And doing what's right
I believe in the bible and standing to fight
I believe in solid principals
I believe in peace
I believe in being kind at the least
I believe in giving grace
And doing a good deed
I may not have everything the world says I
should but I have everything I need
I have what's important
Yes indeed

I have a roof over my head and food to eat
I have a shirt on my back and shoes on my feet
I have love and laughter
I have forgiveness
I have what matters
Forget all the rest
I have much to be grateful for
I'm blessed
I have faith
And hope is a must
My children love God and Jesus
What else could I ask for
I have everything and so much more

www.ingramcontent.com/pod-product-compliance
Lightning Source LLC
LaVergne TN
LVHW021328200726
843509LV00014B/2441